MONSTERS, MAGIC AND MAKE-BELIEVE

A Whole-Language Approach To Teaching Thinking Skills

Written by
Vowery Dodd Carlile

Illustrated by
Karen Neulinger and James Uttel

Educational Impressions

ISBN 1-56644-956-1

Printed in USA.

Contents

FOREWORD

Children around the world enjoy tales about monsters and magic. *Monsters, Magic and Make-believe: A Whole-Language Approach to Teaching Thinking Skills* presents ten popular children's stories, which are used to teach critical and creative thinking skills. Each unit begins with a summary of the story and questions from Bloom's *Taxonomy.** Following these questions are independent project ideas developed to encourage creative thinking and writing.

The units may be used in any order. Begin each by reading the story to the class. Ask any or all Bloom questions based upon the story. Then choose some or all of the projects for the students to complete.

After all the books have been read, allow the children to do the puzzles and other ''Just for Fun'' activities found at the end of the units.

Vowery Dodd Carlile

---

* Benjamin Bloom, *Taxonomy of Educational Objectives*, (New York: David McKay Company, Inc., 1956).

INTRODUCTION

There are many advantages to using children's books in teaching reading, writing and thinking skills. *Monsters, Magic and Make-believe: A Whole-Language Approach to Teaching Thinking Skills* includes ten well-loved, fantastical tales about monsters, dragons, and magic. These subjects are exciting to children of all ages. It seems that fantasy, dragons and magic create a dream land where children can imagine themselves in all types of adventures. As our society has changed, we have gotten away from encouraging our children to pretend and to create their own little worlds. This is a healthy part of their lives. By using *Monsters, Magic and Make-believe,* youngsters can become characters in these stories and experience adventures in make-believe lands.

Each unit includes activities to promote critical and creative thinking. They include questions based upon Bloom's *Taxonomy of Educational Objectives,** independent research and planning activities, and creative writing projects.

Bloom divided cognitive development into six main levels: knowledge, comprehension, application, analysis, synthesis, and evaluation. Most of the questions presented to students fall into the first two categories, knowledge and comprehension. The highest levels are seldom used; they are more difficult to write and, because they have no definite answer, are more difficult to evaluate. Understanding Bloom's Taxonomy will help you provide for your students more and better opportunities to think critically. The following is a brief description of the cognitive levels according to Bloom's taxonomy.

Knowledge: This level involves the **simple recall** of facts stated directly.

Comprehension: The student must **understand** what has been read at this level. It will not be stated directly.

Application: The student uses knowledge that has been learned and **applies** it to a new situation. He/She must understand that knowledge in order to use it.

Analysis: The student **breaks down** learned knowledge into small parts and analyzes it. He/She will pick out unique characteristics and compare them with other ideas.

Synthesis: The student can now **create** something new and original from the acquired knowledge. This level involves a great deal of creativity.

Evaluation: The student makes a **judgment** and must be able to back up that judgment.

Independent projects can be written to cover any subject using verbs that encourage responses from each of the six categories. These verbs can be used to design independent projects as well as to write your own higher-level questions in any subject area. Verbs for each of the categories include the following:

Knowledge: list, know, define, relate, repeat, recall, specify, tell, name

Comprehension: recognize, restate, explain, describe, summarize, express, review, discuss, identify, locate, report, retell

Application: demonstrate, interview, simulate, dramatize, experiment, show, use, employ, operate, exhibit, apply, calculate, solve, illustrate

Analysis: compare, examine, categorize, group, test, inventory, probe, analyze, discover, arrange, scrutinize, organize, contrast, classify, survey

Synthesis: plan, develop, invent, predict, propose, produce, arrange, formulate, construct, incorporate, originate, create, prepare, design, set up

Evaluation: value, recommend, evaluate, criticize, estimate, decide, conclude, predict, judge, compare, rate, measure, select, infer

These verbs can be used to design independent projects as well as to write your own higher-level questions in any subject area. Below is an example of the chart that I use when creating the independent projects in my books. I have also included a copy for you to reproduce and use when designing your own projects.

CATEGORY	VERB	TOPIC	PROJECT
Synthesis	Invent	*Where the Wild Things Are*	A new way for Max to travel.

By incorporating these question-and-project strategies into the curriculum, every child will be given the opportunity to be a creative thinker.

* Benjamin Bloom, *Taxonomy of Educational Objectives,* (New York: David McKay Company, Inc., 1956).

Independent Projects Chart

CATEGORY	VERB	TOPIC	PROJECT

Where the Wild Things Are

by Maurice Sendak

This story has been entertaining children for many years—through T.V. specials as well as through Maurice Sendak's award-winning book itself. *Where the Wild Things Are* gives children the opportunity to put themselves in Max's place and to travel to distant lands of dreams and fantasies.

Begin by discussing monsters. Ask the following questions:

1. Name some monsters.

2. Would you like to command an army of monsters? Why or why not?

3. What would your monsters do?

Read the story *Where the Wild Things Are* to the children. When you have completed the story, discuss the questions based upon Bloom's Taxonomy with them. Then choose some or all of the projects and have the youngsters work on them independently or in groups.

Questions & Activities Based Upon Bloom's Taxonomy

Where the Wild Things Are

Knowledge:
1. What kind of suit did Max wear?
2. Describe the changes that took place in Max's room.
3. What did Max travel in when he crossed the ocean?

Comprehension:
1. Why was Max's mother mad at him?
2. How did Max control the Wild Things?
3. Who was the main character of this story?

Application:
1. Explain what *mischief* means.
2. Do you know anyone like Max? Tell about him or her and explain how they are alike.
3. What three questions would you like to ask Max about his life?

Analysis:
1. Compare Max's mother to your mother. How are they alike and how are they different?
2. Categorize the Wild Things.
3. Explain why the Wild Things looked to Max as their leader.

Synthesis:
1. Create another place for Max to visit. Tell about it.
2. What might have happened if Max's boat had been blown off course on his way home?
3. Invent a new way for Max to travel.

Evaluation:
1. Could this story really have happened? Why or why not?
2. Recommend this book to a friend. Give three reasons why someone would want to read this book.
3. What kind of person is Max? Give reasons for your answer.

Monsters, Good and Bad

List all the monsters you can think of.

_____

_____

_____

_____

_____

_____

_____

_____

**Now categorize them into
Good Monsters and Bad Monsters.**

Good Monsters

_____

_____

_____

_____

_____

_____

Bad Monsters

_____

_____

_____

_____

_____

_____

**Write a poem
from the
Wild Things
to Max.**

To Max

Write a letter to Max's mother.
Tell her why Max should not be
allowed to travel around the world.

Dear

Design a
cover for
a new book about
Max's journey.

WHERE THE WILD THINGS ARE

Create song lyrics to go along with the story. Use a well known tune to help you with your song.

What song will you use?

Write your lyrics here.

Draw and label a map of Max's travels.

START

Suppose
you were Max.

Write about how you felt as you approached the island of the Wild Things.

_____

_____

_____

_____

_____

_____

_____

_____

_____

_____

_____

_____

_____

_____

The Popcorn Dragon

by Jane Thayer

The Popcorn Dragon is a good book to use to teach a lesson about our need to be accepted by others. It is also a good means of pointing out that showing off is not the way to accomplish this goal.

Dexter wants his friends to like him and in order to get their attention, he shows off. However, his friends soon tire of his behavior and he ends up losing them. He doesn't get them back until he stops showing off.

Begin by discussing the fact that we all need to be accepted; elicit from the children that people often show off in order to get people to notice them. Ask the following questions:

1. Why do some people show off?

2. Did you ever show off? Why?

3. Did showing off have the result you had wanted?

4. Do you know people who show off a lot? How do you react to their behavior? Do you like it or does it bother you?

Read the story *The Popcorn Dragon* to the children. When you have completed the story, discuss the questions based upon Bloom's Taxonomy with them. Then choose some or all of the projects and have the youngsters work on them independently or in groups.

Questions & Activities Based Upon Bloom's Taxonomy

The Popcorn Dragon

Knowledge:
1. Describe Dexter's appearance.
2. Name Dexter's friends.
3. Tell how Dexter felt when his friends wouldn't let him play with them.

Comprehension:
1. What was unique (different) about Dexter?
2. How did Dexter use his hot breath?
3. Why did Dexter's friends get upset with him?

Application:
1. If Dexter had been your friend, how would you have reacted to his behavior?
2. Demonstrate some of your talents to the class.
3. Dramatize a scene in which Dexter was showing off in front of his friends.

Analysis:
1. Compare Dexter to one of your good friends. How are they alike and how are they different?
2. Examine Dexter's personality. List three of his personality traits.
3. Make an inventory of all the possible ways Dexter could use his hot breath.

Synthesis:
1. Create a business in which Dexter could use his hot breath to make products or provide a service.
2. What might have happened if Dexter had not discovered that he could pop popcorn. How could he have gotten his friends back?
3. Create a talent for each of Dexter's friends. Describe how the talents could be used.

Evaluation:
1. Was it right for Dexter's friends to treat him as they did? Why or why not?
2. What lesson can be learned from this story? How can you apply it to your life?
3. Would you recommend this story to a friend? Why or why not?

Attention-Getters

List all the ways you can think of to get attention.

_____

_____

_____

_____

_____

_____

_____

_____

_____

_____

Categorize your ideas into
Appropriate and Non-Appropriate Behavior.

Appropriate Behavior	Non-Appropriate Behavior
_____	_____
_____	_____
_____	_____
_____	_____
_____	_____
_____	_____

Write three questions you would like to ask Dexter about being a dragon.

1.

2.

3.

A legend is a story that has been handed down from earlier times. Although it is believed by many people, it cannot be proved true.

Investigate two legends about dragons. Report your findings to the class.

NOTE: You may have to ask your teacher or librarian to help you find the legends.

**Write a conversation between
Dexter and one of his friends.
Have them discuss how
to set up their new business.**

Dexter: _____

_____

Friend: _____

_____

Dexter: _____

_____

Friend: _____

_____

Dexter: _____

_____

Friend: _____

_____

Develop a poster to advertise Dexter's Famous Popcorn.

Use popcorn to design a picture that shows something about Dexter.

Create a new story about Dexter.

Write about another way Dexter might win friends without showing off.

_____
_____
_____
_____
_____
_____
_____
_____
_____
_____
_____
_____
_____

Hershel and the Hanukkah Goblins

by Eric Kimmel

Hershel and the Hanukkah Goblins is a story based upon the Jewish holiday Hanukkah; therefore, it is best if this unit is done just before or during the celebration of the holiday. Before reading the story to the children, read to them the history of Hanukkah, which is found at the back of the book. It will give more meaning to the story if youngsters understand the vocabulary used. You may wish to elicit from the children that although Hanukkah and Christmas often are celebrated about the same time of year, the two holidays have little in common.

Begin by discussing the fact that different cultures celebrate different holidays. Ask the following questions:

1. Does anyone in the class already know the story of Hanukkah? If so, would you like to tell the story to the class?

2. What is a menorah?

3. What is a goblin?

4. Hanukkah is a religious holiday. Name three or more holidays that you celebrate that are not religious.

Read the story *Hershel and the Hanukkah Goblins* to the children. When you have completed the story, discuss the questions based upon Bloom's Taxonomy with them. Then choose some or all of the projects and have the youngsters work on them independently or in groups.

Questions & Activities Based Upon Bloom's Taxonomy

Hershel and the Hanukkah Goblins

Knowledge:
1. Where was Hershel from?
2. How many Hanukkah candles are lit each night?
3. What did the townspeople give to Hershel to eat?

Comprehension:
1. Explain why no Hanukkah candles could be seen in the townspeople's windows when Hershel arrived.
2. Describe a goblin.
3. Why didn't the townspeople expect to see Hershel again?

Application:
1. Is there a haunted house near your home? Tell about it.
2. Does Hanukkah remind you of any other holiday? In what way?
3. Explain why the goblin couldn't get his hand out of the pickle jar. Demonstrate your explanation to the class.

Analysis:
1. Compare the smallest goblin to the King of Goblins. How are they alike and how are they different?
2. Arrange a test to prove that ghosts and goblins do not really exist.
3. Find out how Hanukkah came about.

Synthesis:
1. Create another goblin. Illustrate a picture of it.
2. Produce a menu that the townspeople might have prepared for Hershel on his return.
3. Suppose you won all the goblin's gold. What would you do with it?

Evaluation:
1. If you were Hershel, how would you have felt when you saw the King of Goblins? What would you have done?
2. Which goblin did you think was the scariest? Why?
3. Suppose a whole town were depending upon you to destroy evil and that there was great danger. How would you react?

20

Holiday Foods

Fried foods, especially potato pancakes, are often served on Hanukkah. Think of the different kinds of food your family eats on holidays. List all the holiday foods you can think of. Next to each write the name of the holiday or holidays on which it is served.

_____

_____

_____

_____

_____

_____

_____

_____

_____

_____

_____

_____

_____

_____

Which of the above foods is your favorite? Put a check next to that food.

Create another game in which Hershel could have tricked a goblin.

Explain the rules of your game here.

Draw a picture of the game being played.

Write three questions for an interview with the King of the Goblins.

1.

2.

3.

Create a tabletop or bulletin board display.
Choose at least 5 different holidays.
Decide upon a symbol to represent each.
Use your symbols and other pictures
to create your display.

**Plan another way
that Hershel could have
tricked a goblin.
Write a paragraph about it.**

Draw a picture to illustrate your paragraph.

Write a song about Hershel's great victory over the King of the Goblins. Use a tune you already know and add your own words to it.

Write
a new ending
for the story.

Suppose Hershel had not been able to trick the King Goblin into lighting all the Hanukkah candles. How might the story have been different? _____

_____

_____

_____

_____

_____

_____

_____

_____

_____

Princess Furball

retold by Charlotte Huck

Children dream of fairy tales and their stories of princes and princesses, kings and queens. *Princess Furball* is fairy tale with a theme like that of the Cinderella story. It is similar to the English *Catskin* and to the Grimms Brothers' *Many Furs* or *Thousand Furs*. Tell the children that you are going to read them a fairy tale about a princess.

Before reading the story to the children, ask them to think about the other fairy tales they know. Ask the following questions:

1. What is a fairy tale?

2. Name another fairy tale with a princess in it.

3. Are fairy tales real or make-believe?

4. What is your favorite fairy tale?

Read the story *Princess Furball* to the children. When you have completed the story, discuss the questions based upon Bloom's Taxonomy with them. Then choose some or all of the projects and have the youngsters work on them independently or in groups.

Questions & Activities Based Upon Bloom's Taxonomy

Princess Furball

Knowledge:
1. What was the color of the Princess's hair?
2. Name the three things Princess Furball asked her father to give her.
3. How did the Princess carry her gifts when she ran away?

Comprehension:
1. Explain how Princess Furball got her name.
2. Why did the Princess run away?
3. Tell how Furball tricked the handsome young king.

Application:
1. Describe a typical meal at the king's castle. Then describe a meal at your home. What do the two meals have in common?
2. Dramatize how Furball must have looked when the king's men found her.
3. If you were Furball, what might you have taken with you when you ran away?

Analysis:
1. Compare Furball's life as a princess to her life as a servant. How are they alike and how are they different?
2. Classify the social order of the kingdom; begin with the servants and end with the king.
3. Read the story of *Cinderella* and compare it to this story. How are they alike and how are they different?

Synthesis:
1. Suppose Furball's father had succeeded in forcing her to marry the ogre. How would her life have been different?
2. Create another boyfriend for Furball. How might she decide which one to marry?
3. Pretend you are the cook. How might you convince the king that you—and not Furball—made his favorite soup?

Evaluation:
1. Was it right for Furball to run away from home? Explain.
2. Choose a favorite character in the story and tell why he or she is your favorite.
3. Did you like this story? Give reasons for your opinion.

Favorite Fairy Tales

List all the fairy tales you can think of.

_____

_____

_____

_____

_____

_____

_____

_____

_____

_____

Now think of ways to categorize them. For example, you might group together all the fairy tales that have a princess in the story. You may include the tales in more than one group.

Pretend to be a newscaster at Furball's wedding. Prepare a news report.

Design a royal invitation to the wedding.

Pretend you are Furball's father. From his point of view, write a paragraph describing how you felt when you found out that your daughter had run away.

_____

_____

_____

_____

_____

_____

_____

_____

_____

_____

_____

Sketch a picture of the castle where Furball and her husband will live.

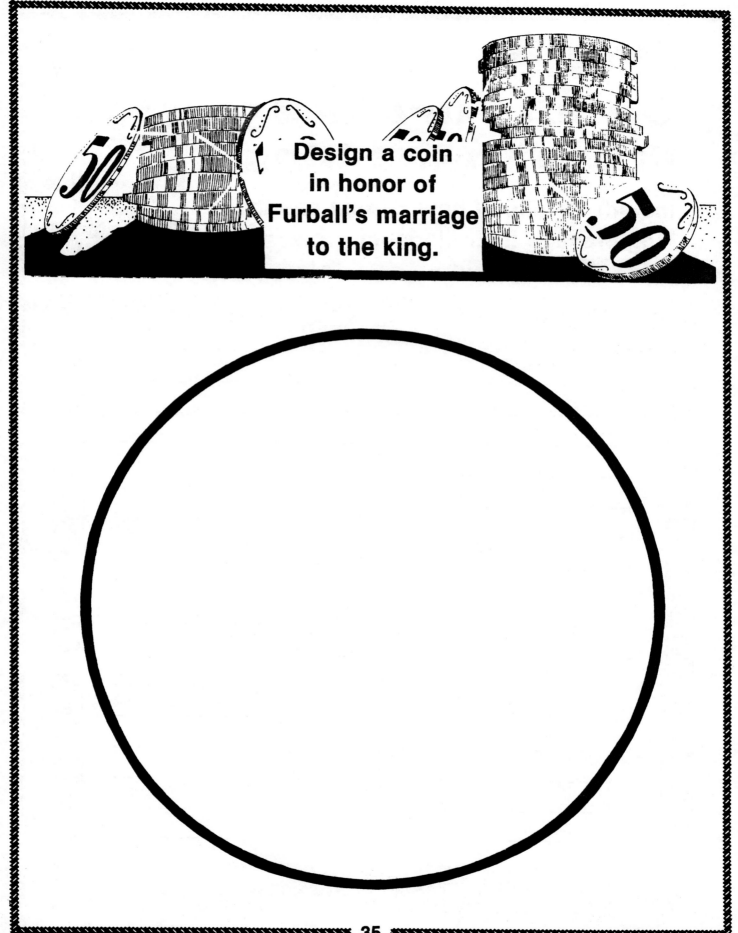

**Design a coin
in honor of
Furball's marriage
to the king.**

Write about Furball's life with the king.

Include details of how Furball and the king manage their kingdom.

_____

_____

_____

_____

_____

_____

_____

_____

_____

_____

_____

_____

_____

_____

_____

Sylvester and the Magic Pebble

by William Steig

Sylvester and the Magic Pebble is a Caldecott Award-winning tale about a donkey who inadvertently turns himself into a rock. This is wonderful book to encourage children to discuss their feelings. It can also be used to teach important value lessons.

Begin by discussing what would happen if a child became lost. Ask the following questions:

1. How could you get lost?

2. What would you do if you became lost?

3. Where could you go for help?

When you have finished this discussion, discuss values. Ask questions such as these:

1. If you could buy anything in the world, what would you buy?

2. If you had a chance to improve the world with your money, what would you do?

3. How might being rich affect you?

4. Would you be the same person if you could have anything you wanted at any time?

Read the story *Sylvester and the Magic Pebble* to the children. When you have completed the story, discuss the questions based upon Bloom's Taxonomy with them. Then choose some or all of the projects and have the youngsters work on them independently or in groups.

Questions & Activities Based Upon Bloom's Taxonomy

Sylvester and the Magic Pebble

Knowledge:
1. What was Sylvester's favorite thing to do?
2. What did Sylvester find?
3. List two things Sylvester wished for.

Comprehension:
1. How did Mr. and Mrs. Duncan try to find Sylvester?
2. Explain how Sylvester turned into a rock.
3. How might Sylvester have kept from changing into a rock?

Application:
1. If you found a magic pebble, what would you wish for?
2. How would your mother and father feel if you became lost? How might they find you?
3. If you were lost, how would you find your way home?

Analysis:
1. Compare Sylvester's feelings as a donkey to his feelings as a rock. How are they alike and how are they different?
2. What questions might the police ask Sylvester's parents that would help them find Sylvester?
3. Organize a hunt for Sylvester. Describe how you would go about it.

Synthesis:
1. Suppose Sylvester had wished to be a bird. How might the story have been different?
2. Pretend that you are Sylvester. Explain how you feel as you change from the rock back to yourself.
3. How could Sylvester have used the pebble to create a better world?

Evaluation:
1. Would a magic pebble change your feelings and beliefs? Describe how it might change you.
2. If you had a magic pebble and could go anywhere in the world, where would you go? Why?
3. Suppose you had the choice of making the world a better place or becoming rich. Which would you choose? Why?

I Wish . . .

You have just found a magic ring. Anything you wish will come true! List all the wishes you will make.

_____

_____

_____

_____

_____

_____

_____

_____

_____

_____

Now suppose you could only have one of those wishes. Which one would you choose? Explain why.

_____

_____

_____

On another sheet of paper draw a picture that shows that wish coming true.

Write a "Missing Donkey" report for the back of a milk carton. Be sure to describe Sylvester and to tell as many details of his disappearance as you can. Draw a picture of him in the space provided.

MILK

OPEN ▶

MILK

· HAVE YOU ·
SEEN?
· SYLVESTER ·

✳ DESCRIPTION ✳

HEIGHT: _____
WEIGHT: _____
EYE COLOR: _____

DETAILS: _____

Create a board game
to go along with the story.

ON THE AIR

Pretend you are a reporter for the local radio station. Record your report describing the missing donkey story.

W·SLY

Design a comic strip that shows several ways in which Sylvester could use the magic pebble.

ADVENTURES OF SYLVESTER AND THE MAGIC PEBBLE

Create puppets of the main characters in the story. Use paper bags, scraps of construction paper, and so on. Use your puppets to retell the story.

Add another character to the story.

Your new character is trying to steal the magic pebble. Describe what Sylvester and his family do to protect it.

_____

_____

_____

_____

_____

_____

_____

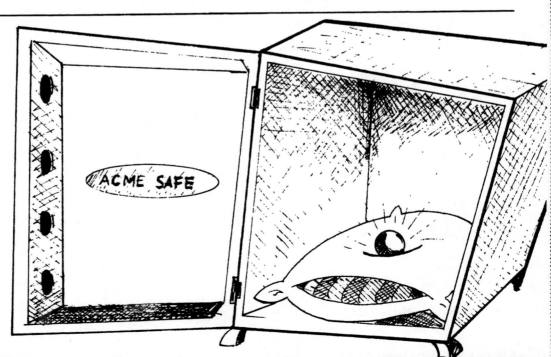

ACME SAFE

Magic Growing Powder

by Janet Quin-Harkin

Children have fun imagining what it would be like to have magic powers. *Magic Growing Powder* is a story about a king whose dream is to be tall. He is willing to sacrifice his kingdom for his dream and is tempted by a magic growing powder, which two tricksters bring him. Due to his daughter's cleverness, he does not lose his kingdom and in the end he realizes that there is nothing wrong with being short.

Begin this unit by telling the children that you are going to read them a story about a king who wanted so badly to be tall that he was willing to give up his kingdom to get his wish. Discuss what things the children would like to change about themselves. Also elicit from them that we often convince ourselves to believe what we want to believe. Ask the following questions:

1. If you could, what would you change about yourself?

2. What would you be willing to give up in order to make the change?

3. Have you ever believed that something was true even though you should have known better? Was it because you wanted it to be true?

Read the story *Magic Growing Powder* to the children. When you have completed the story, discuss the questions based upon Bloom's Taxonomy with them. Then choose some or all of the projects and have the youngsters work on them independently or in groups.

Questions & Activities Based Upon Bloom's Taxonomy

Magic Growing Powder

Knowledge:
1. What did the king spend all his time trying to do?
2. What caused King Max to turn green?
3. How long did it take for the magic growing powder to work?

Comprehension:
1. List some ways King Max tried to solve his height problem.
2. Explain how the magic growing powder worked.
3. Why did Princess Penny want to test the powder?

Application:
1. How would you use the magic growing powder?
2. Illustrate a way King Max could look taller.
3. What lesson can you learn from King Max's mistake? How can this help you?

Analysis:
1. Compare short people to tall people. How do they feel about their height. Conduct a survey to support your findings.
2. How is your life different from King Max's and Princess Penny's lives?
3. Compose a questionnaire that you will use to prove that being short has advantages.

Synthesis:
1. Create another way to test the magic growing powder.
2. Suppose King Max had not been convinced that the magic growing powder was fake. How might the story have been different?
3. Design a wedding invitation for Princess Penny's future wedding.

Evaluation:
1. Was Princess Penny a very smart daughter? Explain.
2. If you were short, would you try the magic growing powder? Why or why not?
3. Recommend this book to a friend. Give three reasons for your recommendation.

Things I Would Change

List all the things you would want to change about yourself. Think of all your traits—not just the physical ones!

_____

_____

_____

_____

_____

_____

_____

_____

_____

_____

_____

_____

Now suppose you could change only one thing. Which one would you choose? Explain why.

_____

_____

_____

On another sheet of paper draw a picture that shows how you would be different.

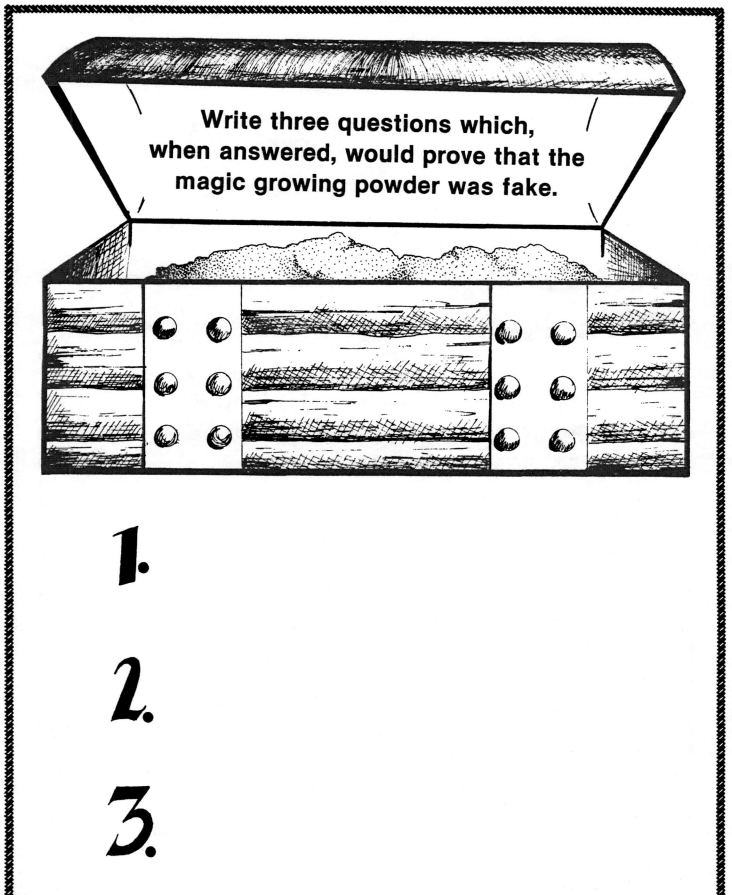

Write three questions which, when answered, would prove that the magic growing powder was fake.

1.

2.

3.

Design a new costume for King Max.

Create a card game or a board game
to go along with the story.

SHORT IS BEAUTIFUL

dog who is kidnapped from his

**You have decided to
market the magic growing powder.
Write a newspaper advertisement
that will encourage
people to buy the product.**

Design paper plate puppets to represent King Max and Princess Penny. Use the puppets to retell the story.

53

Write a poem from King Max to his daughter.

The poem is to thank Princess Penny for saving the king from making a great mistake.

_____

_____

_____

_____

_____

_____

_____

_____

_____

_____

_____

_____

_____

_____

_____

The Paper Bag Princess

by Robert N. Munsch

The Paper Bag Princess is about a princess who is forced into wearing a paper bag because a dragon has burned her clothes and stolen her prince. She tricks the dragon into giving back her prince so that they can marry. In return for her efforts, however, the prince criticizes the princess for her appearance! The princess tells the prince that she doesn't want to marry him after all.

This is a good story to encourage a discussion about not judging people by their appearance. Ask the following questions:

1. Do you ever judge people by the way they look?

2. Were you ever wrong in your first impression about someone?

3. How should you judge people?

This book also provides the basis for a discussion about showing appreciation for the things people do for us. Ask the following questions:

1. Did you ever do something for someone who then complained about the way you did it? How did that make you feel?

2. How do you feel when people show that they appreciate what you did for them?

Read the story *The Paper Bag Princess* to the children. When you have completed the story, discuss the questions based upon Bloom's Taxonomy with them. Then choose some or all of the projects and have the youngsters work on them independently or in groups.

Questions & Activities Based Upon Bloom's Taxonomy

The Paper Bag Princess

Knowledge:
1. Who is Elizabeth?
2. List two things left on the dragon's tail.
3. How many forests did the dragon burn?

Comprehension:
1. What happened to Elizabeth's clothes?
2. Why did the dragon steal Ronald?
3. Explain how Elizabeth tricked the dragon?

Application:
1. What would you do if you had no clothes to wear?
2. Suggest where the princess might go to get more clothes instead of wearing the bag.
3. Act out the scene in which the dragon storms in and burns all of Elizabeth's clothes.

Analysis:
1. Compare this dragon to the one in *The Popcorn Dragon*. How are they alike and how are they different?
2. Arrange for a test for Ronald to prove his love for Elizabeth.
3. Interpret Elizabeth's feelings toward Ronald at the end of the story as compared to her feelings for him at the beginning of the story.

Synthesis:
1. Design a fashionable paper bag for the princess to wear—one that would show that she is a princess.
2. What other way could Elizabeth have tricked the dragon into giving Ronald back?
3. Plan a meal the princess could offer to the dragon to replace Ronald.

Evaluation:
1. Would Ronald have been a good husband if Elizabeth had married him? Explain your answer.
2. Imagine that you are Elizabeth. Tell how you feel when Ronald criticizes the way you look after you have saved his life. Explain why you feel this way.
3. Pretend to be Ronald. Explain why you reacted the way you did to Elizabeth's appearance.

From Paper Bags

Suppose you just found a pile of old, but clean, paper bags. List all the things you could make from them.

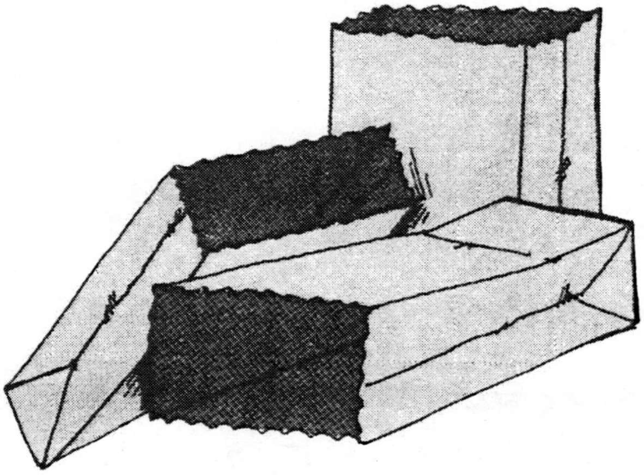

_____
_____
_____
_____
_____
_____
_____
_____
_____
_____
_____
_____
_____
_____

Now choose one of those things and draw a picture.

If possible, make what you have drawn.

Write a letter to the editor of a newspaper. Explain why dragons should have the same rights as humans.

Dear Editor,

_____
_____
_____
_____
_____
_____
_____
_____
_____
_____
_____
_____

**Choreograph, or arrange, a dance
that the princess could use
to get the dragon's attention.**

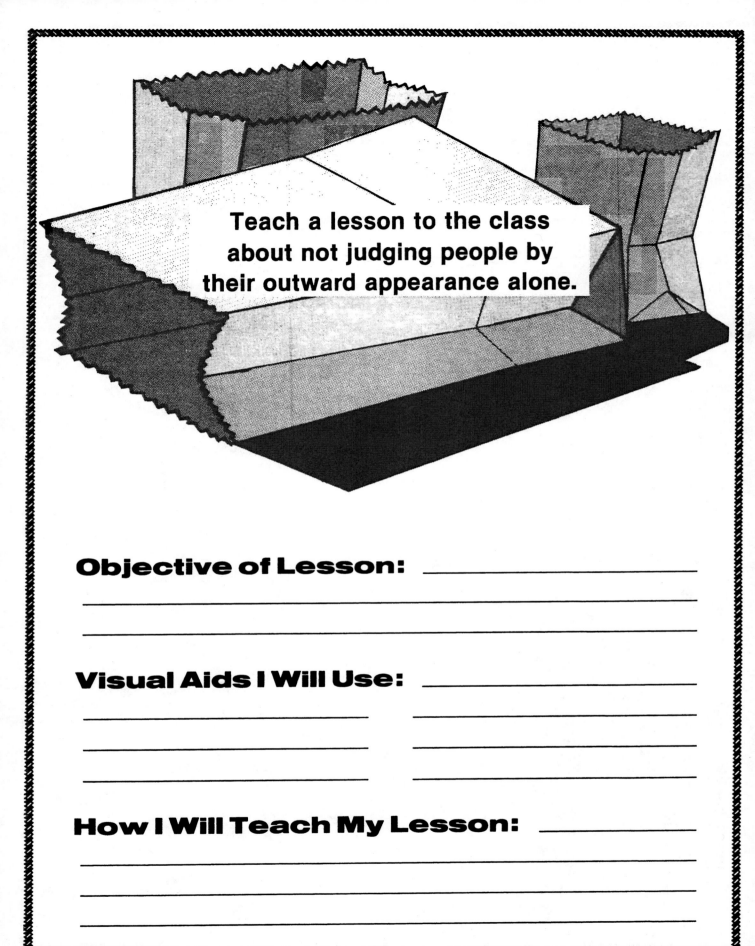

Teach a lesson to the class about not judging people by their outward appearance alone.

Objective of Lesson: _____

_____

_____

Visual Aids I Will Use: _____

_____ _____

_____ _____

_____ _____

How I Will Teach My Lesson: _____

_____

_____

_____

**Create a bulletin board display
to go along with the story.**

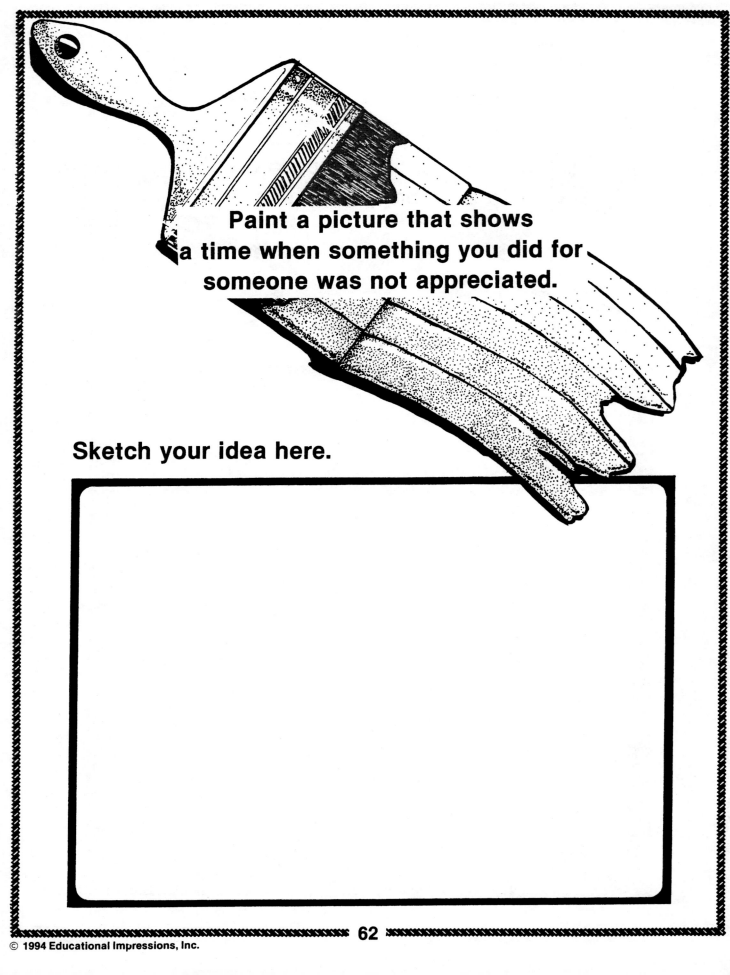

**Paint a picture that shows
a time when something you did for
someone was not appreciated.**

Sketch your idea here.

Write
a story about Elizabeth's life after she left Ronald.

Illustrate your story.

_____

_____

_____

_____

_____

_____

_____

_____

_____

_____

_____

_____

_____

_____

_____

_____

_____

_____

_____

Alexander and the Wind-up Mouse

by Leo Lionni

Alexander and the Wind-up Mouse is a heartwarming story about the friendship that evolves between a live mouse and a wind-up toy mouse. In the story one mouse makes great sacrifices to save his friend.

Begin the unit by discussing what friendship is and what it takes to be a good friend. Ask the following questions:

1. What qualities do you look for in a friend?

2. Are you a good friend?

3. Can good friends ever get mad at each other?

Read the story *Alexander and the Wind-up Mouse* to the children. When you have completed the story, discuss the questions based upon Bloom's Taxonomy with them. Then choose some or all of the projects and have the youngsters work on them independently or in groups.

Questions & Activities Based Upon Bloom's Taxonomy

Alexander and the Wind-up Mouse

Knowledge:
1. What did Alexander want when everyone chased him away?
2. What was the name of the wind-up mouse?
3. In whose room did Alexander discover the wind-up mouse?

Comprehension:
1. Explain how the wind-up mouse worked.
2. Why did Alexander have to bring the lizard a purple pebble?
3. Why did Alexander want to be changed into a wind-up mouse?

Application:
1. Have you ever had a favorite toy? Describe it.
2. What do you do with your toys when you get tired of them?
3. If you could change into something, what would you become? Why? Would you want to stay that way forever?

Analysis:
1. Compare Willy and Alexander. How are they alike and how are they different?
2. Write three facts that would convince Alexander that it would be better to be a real mouse than a wind-up one.
3. How might Alexander have reacted if Willy had been thrown out with the old toys? Explain your answer.

Synthesis:
1. Create a new home for Willy and Alexander. Describe it.
2. How would the story have been different if Alexander had turned into a wind-up mouse?
3. Describe a way Willy might have convinced Annie not to throw him out with the other old toys.

Evaluation:
1. Which would be better, real or wind-up? Why?
2. Judge Alexander's change of mind when speaking to the lizard.
3. If you could have any pet you wanted, what would you choose? Why?

So Many Toys

List as many different kinds of toys as you can.

_____

_____

_____

_____

_____

_____

_____

_____

_____

_____

_____

Now think of ways to categorize them. For example, you might group together all small toys or all toys that move by themselves. You may include the toys in more than one group.

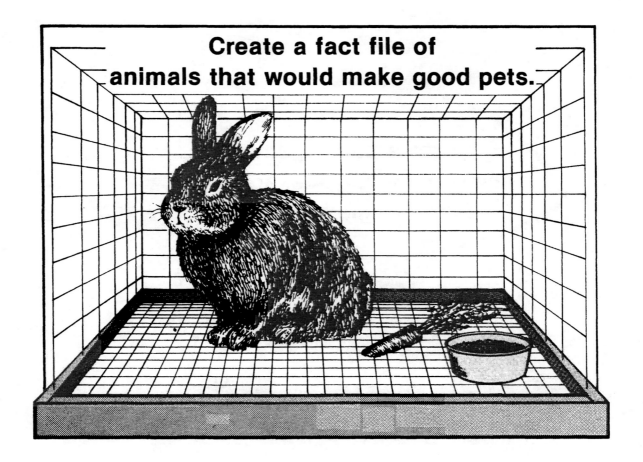

Create a fact file of animals that would make good pets.

Make copies of the fact file form. Use them to record your information.

FACT FILE FORM

SUBJECT: _____

RESOURCE: _____

FACTS:_____

_____

_____

_____

_____

_____

Create a board game
using Willy and Alexander
as the game pieces.

An elegy is a poem that laments the dead. Compose an elegy for toys that have been thrown away.

Now design a tombstone for the toys.

Design a poster that asks people to donate their old toys to poor children.

With a friend, create a pantomime skit that shows how Willy and Alexander met and became friends.

Write
a short story.

In your story Willy rescues Alexander from being caught in a mouse trap.

_____

_____

_____

_____

_____

_____

_____

_____

_____

_____

_____

_____

_____

_____

_____

_____

_____

The Snow Child

retold by Freya Littledale

The Snow Child is a touching story of a man and woman who are very sad because they have no children. When winter comes, they build a snow girl and wish that she were alive. The wife kisses her and the snow girl comes to life. With the warm weather, however, she leaves them, for she must live in the cold all year long. The man and woman are again sad until winter returns, and with it their snow child.

Begin the unit by discussing winter and the things your students like to do in the winter. Ask the following questions:

1. What do you like to do in the winter?

2. Would you like to live in a place that has winter all year long? Why or why not?

3. What don't you like about winter?

4. Did you ever build a snowperson?

Read the story *The Snow Child* to the children. When you have completed the story, discuss the questions based upon Bloom's Taxonomy with them. Then choose some or all of the projects and have the youngsters work on them independently or in groups.

Questions & Activities Based Upon Bloom's Taxonomy

The Snow Child

Knowledge:
1. What were the village children building?
2. What did the old man and woman want?
3. Where did the snow child sleep?

Comprehension:
1. Describe how the old man and woman made the snow child.
2. Why did the snow child have to leave when the snow was gone?
3. What did the snow child teach the village children to do?

Application:
1. Describe some of the things you do in the winter to have fun.
2. If you had a snow child, how would you take care of her?
3. If you were a snow child and had to leave your family during the summer, where would you go?

Analysis:
1. Compare having a child to having a pet. How are they alike and how are they different?
2. Examine the good and bad aspects of having a part-time child.
3. What other story does this remind you of. Discuss the two stories and compare their likes and differences.

Synthesis:
1. Design a way for the snow child to stay in the house with the old couple. It must be comfortable for all three of them.
2. Suppose the snow child had stayed too long with the old man and woman. What might have happened?
3. Create another snow child to keep the snow girl company. Describe him or her.

Evaluation:
1. Would you like to be a snow child? Why or why not?
2. Pretend you are the old man or woman. Describe how you feel when you have to say goodbye to the snow child each summer. Why do you feel this way?
3. Would you recommend this book to a friend? Explain.

Winter Fun

What do people do in the winter? List the different things people do during the cold winter months.

_____

_____

_____

_____

_____

_____

_____

_____

_____

_____

_____

_____

What do you like to do? On a different sheet of paper, draw a picture of you doing your favorite winter activity.

Write directions for building a snowperson. If possible, have someone follow your directions.

Create snowflakes from paper. Make several different designs. Remember, all snowflakes have six sides. You may copy the pattern on this page to start.

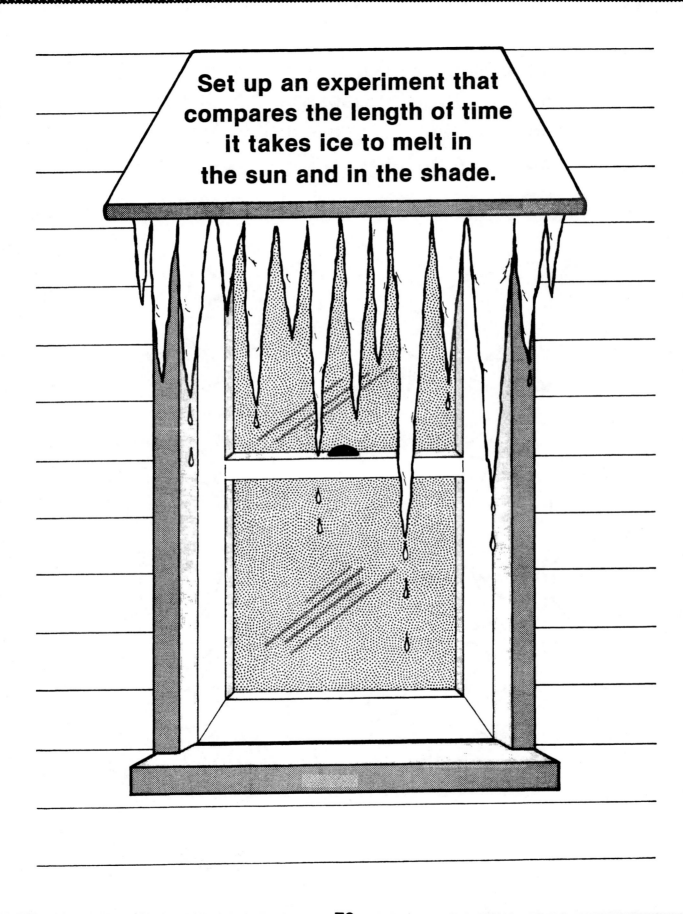

Set up an experiment that compares the length of time it takes ice to melt in the sun and in the shade.

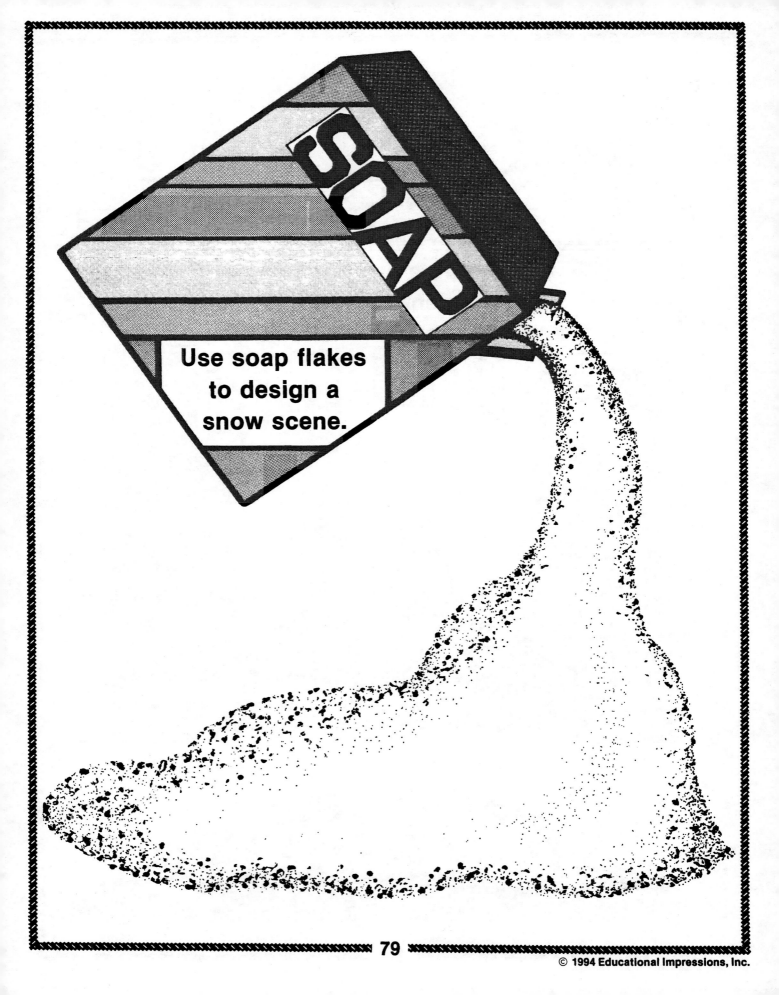

Use soap flakes
to design a
snow scene.

Create a new form of entertainment for you and your friends during the cold winter days.

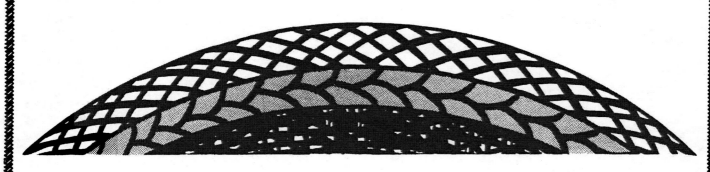

Write
an account of the snow child's travels.

What does she do when she leaves the old couple?

_____

_____

_____

_____

_____

_____

_____

_____

_____

_____

_____

_____

_____

_____

_____

_____

_____

Cloudy with a Chance of Meatballs

by Judi Barrett

Cloudy with a Chance of Meatballs is a humorous story about a town that gets all of its food from the sky. All of its precipitation is in the form of food! No one has to cook anything. Everything is fine until the weather takes a turn for the worse.

Begin the unit by discussing food and where we get it. Ask the following questions:

1. Where does your family get its food?

2. Who does most of the cooking in your home?

3. What would it be like if no one in your family ever had to cook?

4. Have you ever been involved in a food fight? If so, describe it.

5. What would you do if food just started dropping out of the sky?

Read the story *Cloudy with a Chance of Meatballs* to the children. When you have completed the story, discuss the questions based upon Bloom's Taxonomy with them. Then choose some or all of the projects and have the youngsters work on them independently or in groups.

Questions & Activities Based Upon Bloom's Taxonomy

Cloudy with a Chance of Meatballs

Knowledge:
1. What fell on Henry's head?
2. What was the name of the town in Grandpa's story?
3. List some of the foods that fell from the sky.

Comprehension:
1. Explain how the townspeople got their food.
2. Why, do you think, weren't there any food stores in the town?
3. Why couldn't the children go to school?

Application:
1. Describe a typical breakfast in this town and at your house.
2. Would you like your meals to fall from the sky?
3. Plan a menu of meals for one day to fall from the sky. Tell how they will fall.

Analysis:
1. What would be the advantages and disadvantages of having your meals fall from the sky?
2. Explain how food might really fall from the sky.
3. Categorize the food listed in the story into the four basic food groups.

Synthesis:
1. Suppose this story were true. How could it help the hunger problem in the world.
2. Create a business that could use the leftovers.
3. Plan a mass clean-up of all the extra food left after a big storm.

Evaluation:
1. Write a book review of *Cloudy with a Chance of Meatballs* for a magazine. Tell whether or not you would recommend the book and why.
2. Recommend the best way to leave the town. Explain.
3. If you were a resident of Chewandswallow and were given the choice of leaving or staying, which would you choose? Explain.

Food for Thought

List the different kinds of foods you ate this week.

_____

_____

_____

_____

_____

_____

_____

_____

_____

_____

_____

Now categorize the foods. You may include the four basic food groups, but use your imagination to think of other kinds of groups as well. You may put the same food into more than one group.

Pretend you are a
resident of Chewandswallow.
Write an entry in
your diary describing
a typical day.

DIARY

Draw a comic strip
in which food is
falling from the sky.

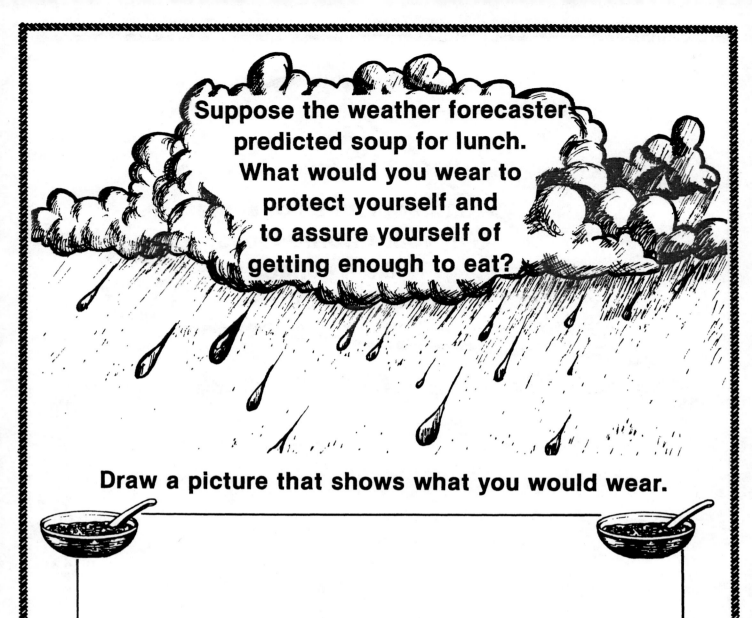

Suppose the weather forecaster predicted soup for lunch. What would you wear to protect yourself and to assure yourself of getting enough to eat?

Draw a picture that shows what you would wear.

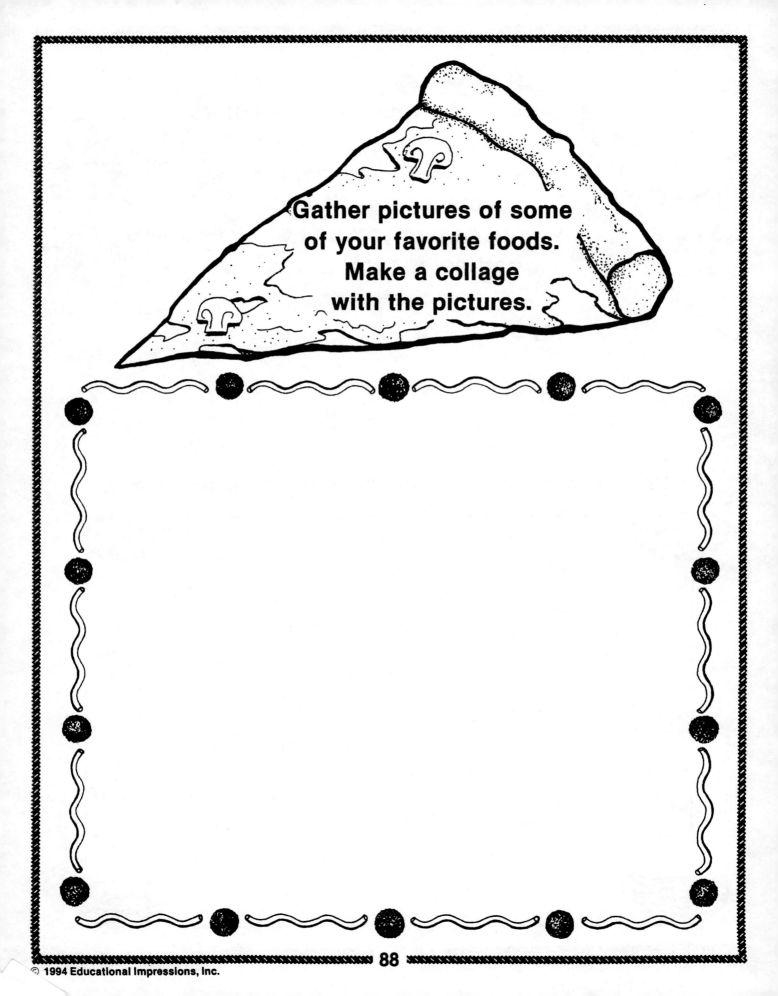

**Gather pictures of some
of your favorite foods.
Make a collage
with the pictures.**

Plan a lesson that teaches about the four basic food groups. Design a poster to go along with your lesson.

Write a song or a poem.

Write about Chewandswallow either before or after it was deserted.

Scrambled Characters

Use the clues to help you unscramble the character names.

1. He turned into a rock.

LYSEVSTER   _ _ _ _ _ _ _ _ _

2. He used his hot breath to make popcorn.

RETXED   _ _ _ _ _ _

3. This mouse had a wind-up friend.

LAEXNADER   _ _ _ _ _ _ _ _ _

4. He was saved from the dragon by the Paper Bag Princess.

DNALOR   _ _ _ _ _ _

5. She returned to the old couple in the winter.

HTE NSWO DLIHC   _ _ _   _ _ _ _   _ _ _ _ _

Bookmarks

Color and decorate your bookmark. Use it when reading your favorite storybook.

Winter Wonderland

It is winter. The Snow Child is trying to find her way home. Help her find her way through the maze. Remember the rule: Do not cross any lines!

Follow the Dots

Connect the dots to complete the picture.

Color your picture. Add details.

Create your own monster.

Write an original story with your monster as the main character. Tell the story from the monster's point of view.

Draw a picture to illustrate your story.

My Wish

Draw a picture of the wish you would make if you had Sylvester's magic pebble.

Make It Bigger

The king gets his wish and grows taller. Now he needs a larger throne!

Look at the throne at the right. Try to make it larger in the squares below.

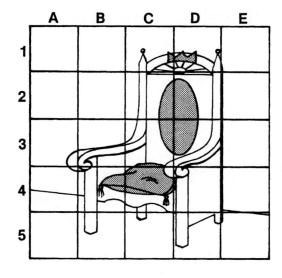

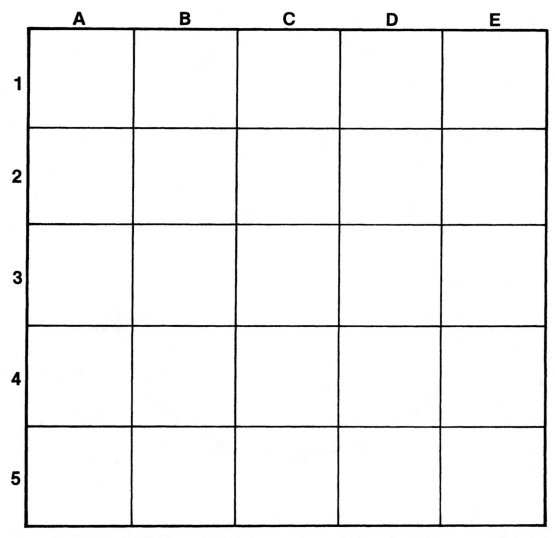

Add the Details

Add details to this snow person and the background to make the picture more interesting. Color your picture.

Color-coded Picture

This picture is to be colored in according to a letter code. The letter "a" will stand for the color blue. That means you will fill in all the spaces marked "a" with blue. Let each of the other letters stand for a different color. Then color in the picture according to your code.

a: blue

b:

c:

d:

e:

f:

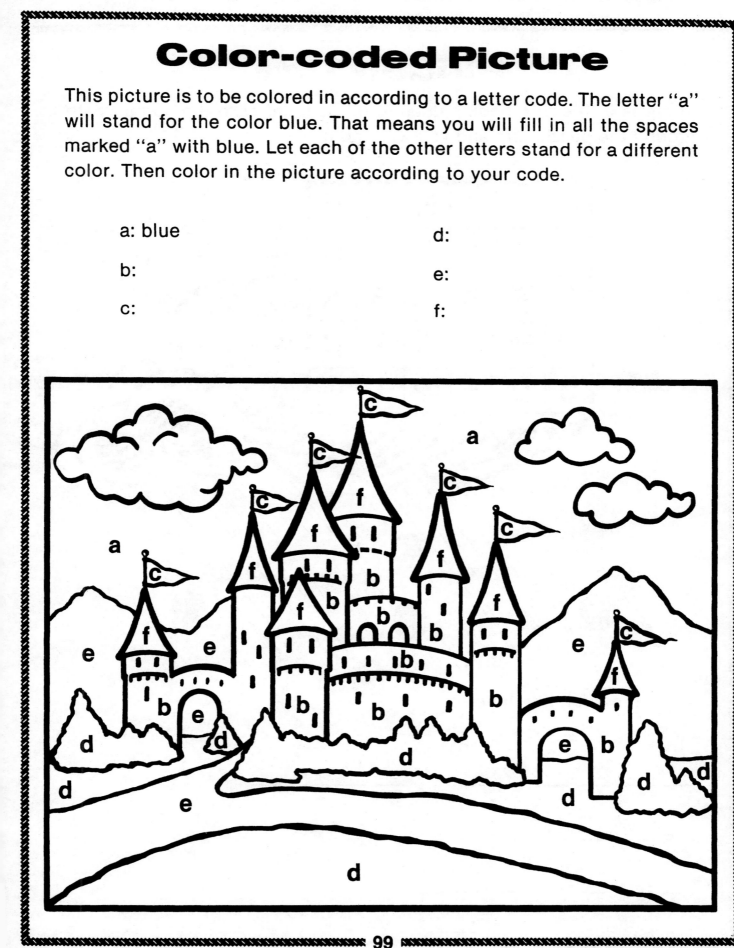

Hidden Title

There is a title of a book hidden in this puzzle. Take the correct path around the puzzle grid and you will find it!

START	E	C	N	A	H
C	O	L	L	A	C
L	F	S	THE END	B	A
O	M	E	A	T	H
U	D	Y	W	I	T

Write the book title here:

_ _ _ _ _ _   _ _ _ _   _

_ _ _ _ _ _   _ _

_ _ _ _ _ _ _ _ _

Monsters, Magic and Make-believe Word Search

See if you can find the words listed below. You may go in a straight line in any direction:

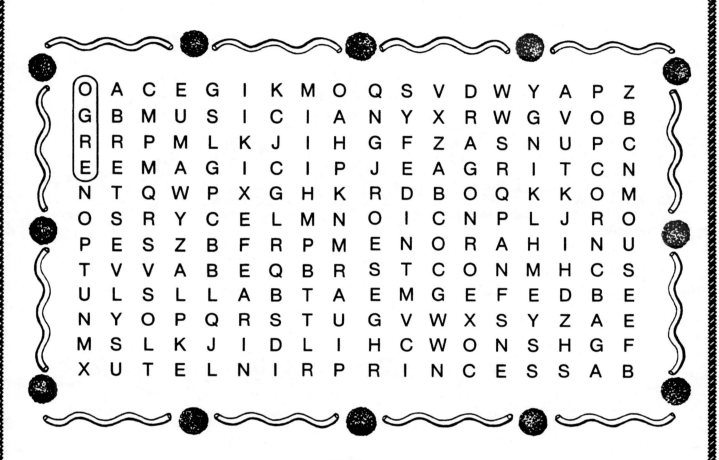

```
O A C E G I K M O Q S V D W Y A P Z
G B M U S I C I A N Y X R W G V O B
R R P M L K J I H G F Z A S N U P C
E E M A G I C I P J E A G R I T C N
N T Q W P X G H K R D B O Q K K O M
O S R Y C E L M N O I C N P L J R O
P E S Z B F R P M E N O R A H I N U
T V V A B E Q B R S T C O N M H C S
U L S L L A B T A E M G E F E D B E
N Y O P Q R S T U G V W X S Y Z A E
M S L K J I D L I H C W O N S H G F
X U T E L N I R P R I N C E S S A B
```

DRAGON	OGRE
KING	PAPER BAG
MAGIC	POPCORN
MEATBALLS	PRINCE
MENORAH	PRINCESS
MOUSE	SNOW CHILD
MUSICIAN	SYLVESTER

Circle the words as you find them. One has been done for you.

Which Is Bigger?

For each set of pictures you must judge the sizes of the objects. For each line write #1 in the box under the smallest object in the set; write #2 in the box under the next smallest object in the set; and so on. The biggest object in each set should have the number 5 in the box.

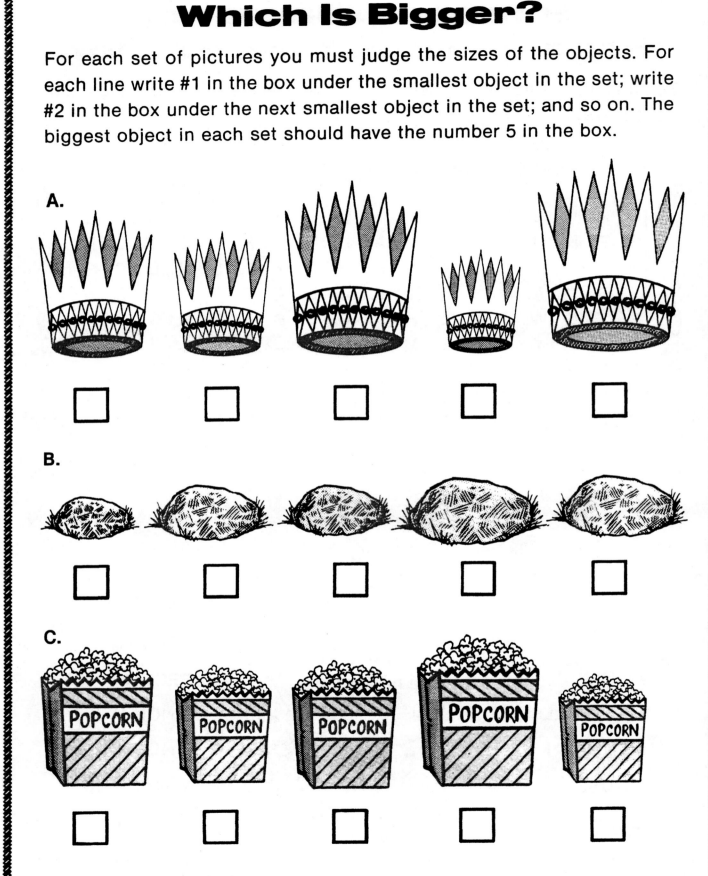

A.

B.

C.

Same and Different

Look carefully at each set of pictures. For each, decide which one is **exactly** like the one on the left. Circle that picture.

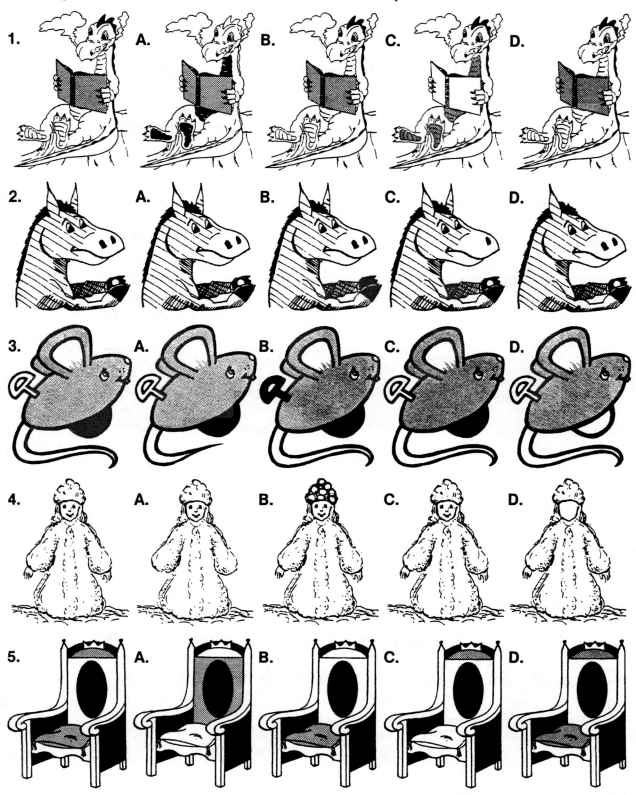

BIBLIOGRAPHY

Barrett, Judi. *Cloudy with a Chance of Meatballs.* New York: Atheneum, 1978.

Barrett, Judi. *Cloudy with a Chance of Meatballs.* New York: Scholastic, Inc., 1989.

Harkin-Quin, Janet. *Magic Growing Powder.* New York: Parents' Magazine Press, 1980.

Huch, Charlotte. *Princess Furball.* New York: Greenwillow Books, 1989.

Huch, Charlotte. *Princess Furball.* New York: Scholastic, Inc., 1989.

Kimmel, Eric. *Hershel and the Hanukkah Goblins.* New York: Holiday House, 1989.

Kimmel, Eric. *Hershel and the Hanukkah Goblins.* New York: Scholastic, Inc., 1990.

Lionni, Leo. *Alexander and the Wind-up Mouse.* New York: Pantheon, 1969.

Lionni, Leo. *Alexander and the Wind-up Mouse.* New York: Scholastic, Inc., 1989.

Littledale, Freya. *The Snow Child.* New York: Scholastic, Inc., , 1989.

Munsch, N. Robert. *The Paper Bag Princess.* Canada: Annich Press LTD, 1980.

Sendak, Maurice. *Where the Wild Things Are.* New York: Harper & Row, 1963.

Steig, William. *Sylvester and the Magic Pebble.* New York: Simon & Schuster, 1969.

Thayer, Jane. *The Popcorn Dragon.* New York: William Morrow and Co., 1953.

Thayer, Jane. *The Popcorn Dragon.* New York: Scholastic, Inc., 1990.

SUPPLEMENTAL READING

Cohen, Daniel. *America's Very Own Monsters.* New York: Dodd, 1982.

Viorst, Judith. *My Mama Says There Aren't Any.* New York: Macmillan, 1973.